Holiday Prospecting for Dollars

A How-To Guide to Help Agents Close More Deals During the Holidays

William May

Copyright © 2017 WillieJMayEnterprises.com

All rights reserved. No part of this book may be reproduced in any form or by any electronic or mechanical means, including information storage and retrieval systems, without permission in writing from the author. The only exception is by a reviewer, who may quote short excerpts in a published review.

©2017 WillieJMayEnterprises

Disclaimer: William J. May is a licensed real estate agent in Torrance, California. Printed in the USA. The information presented herein represents the views of the author as of the date of publication. This book is presented for informational purposes only. This book contains statistical examples.

It is understood, if you use these statistics, you need to know your own market. Real Estate is local, and every market is different. Due to the rate of which conditions change, the author reserves the right to alter and/or update this information based on new conditions. While every attempt has been made to verify the information in this book, neither the author nor his affiliates/partners assume any responsibility for errors, inaccuracies, or omissions. It is understood that the income statements and examples are not intended to represent or guarantee that anyone will achieve the same results. Each individual's success will be determined by his or her desire, dedication, background, skills, knowledge, effort, and motivation to work and follow recommendations. There is no guarantee you will duplicate the results stated. You recognize any business endeavor has an inherent risk for loss of capital.

Get This Book as a Course

http://expiredlistingmastery101.com

- Get This Book as a Course 2
- Introduction 5
- Reset your Mindset 9
  - Energy Suckers 10
  - Keep Life Simple! 11
  - Your Morning Routine 13
  - Exercise 14
- Hot Lead Sources 19
  - Expired Listings 20
  - For Sale by Owners 21
  - FSBO Open Houses 22
  - Sphere of Influence (SOI)/Database 22
- Taking Massive Action 24
  - Focus on the Basics 25
  - Top 10 Reasons Why You Should Sell During the Holidays 28
- The Holiday Game Plan 32
- Expired Listings 34
  - Expired Door Knocking 35
  - Calling the Expired Listings 41
  - Direct Mail Campaigns 48
  - The Expired Follow-Up System 51
- For Sale By Owners 59
  - Identifying the Three Types of FSBOs 60
  - Going After For Sale By Owners 61
  - Calling the For Sale By Owner 64
  - The For Sale by Owner Follow-Up System 67
- For Sale by Owner Open Houses 75

Successful Open House Game Plan	76
Past Clients, SOI, and Your Database	94
Creating Your Database	95
The FORD Technique	101
F Stands for Family	102
O Stands for Occupation	103
R Stands for Recreation	104
D Stands for Dreams	105
Your Year-Round Follow-Up Plan	108
The 5-Step System	108
Email	109
Snail Mail	110
Phone Calls	111
Pop By	113
Special Dates	115
Final Thoughts	118
If you enjoyed this book:	121

Introduction

Ever since I was a child I always looked forward to the holidays, especially Christmas. The night before that magical morning, like every other kid around the world, I couldn't sleep. I was too excited to know what would be waiting for me under the tree that morning. As an adult around the corner from hitting 50, I still have that anxious feeling every year around the holidays.

I guess everyone at some point in their life starts thinking about a career in Real Estate. Fast money, fancy cars, clothes, rubbing shoulders with the rich and famous; I've been dreaming about it since I was in high school watching those late-night Carlton Sheets TV spots.

You remember, don't you?

Well fast forward to late 2011: the economy is in the toilet and we are suffering from the worst recession since the great depression. I was in the middle of a divorce and sold my successful school bus company. I just wanted to walk away from everything, and start a new life. What better way to do that than by doing something I always dreamed of...**Real Estate**.

Lo and behold, nobody told me that Real Estate is not as easy is it looks. Do not get me wrong, **Real Estate is easy, just not an easy business.**

So, as they say "Only the strong survive in Real Estate."

That is exactly why I am writing this book, *Holiday Prospecting for Dollars,* to educate you on proven systems. If you work the system, the system will provide results.

No matter when you pick up this book, Winter, Spring, Summer or Fall, it is a quick start, jump start, meant to get you out of a Real Estate sales slump. Let's face it, most agents are not happy with their production: getting four, ten, twenty-five, maybe a hundred deals a year. You can always do much better for you and your family. That's it...right? Family! That's why we go the extra mile. Dealing with clients who don't appreciate us, long hours at the office, babysitting Open Houses where nobody shows? There's nothing more important than family, so you know how important it is to generate business during the holidays.

Holiday Prospecting for Dollars is designed to get you back into a Real Estate kick ass momentum and to stay there. I'm going to give you some keys to jump start your mindset, your motivation, and your passion to succeed in Real Estate.

1. **Reset Your Mindset** - We need to recalibrate your mindset as a top producer and kick out all those limiting beliefs or excuses that are clouding up what's between your ears.
2. **Hot Lead Sources** - Work on **NOW** leads sources, that will generate business now and for years to come.
3. **Taking Massive Action** - Let's take Grant Cardone's example, and 10x our actions because there's no way in hell you are going to be successful in anything you do if you do not take any action. Being a successful Real Estate Agent is all up to you. When you first start, or when you are getting over a sales slump, you are going to have to work your butt off to get back into high gear. You need a system and a game plan that's going to feed your pipeline and grow your business to new heights.

Throughout this book you will find little Easter eggs that will help you with your business. Little golden nuggets like, videos, interviews, and tools that I use for my prospecting that help me develop my business. I will be sharing with you, and I know if you put forth the effort and the hard work that it takes to succeed, the information provided will help you in your business.

So I would suggest, roll up your sleeves and prepare to put forth 10x action if you're serious about succeeding in Real Estate.

Let me ask you a serious question: how would you feel if you had several closings for the holidays and you have some pending sales for future business to start the New Year off strong?

How would the extra income help you and your family? I don't know about you, but I'll be excited to be kicking Real Estate ass while everyone is coming back from their holiday vacation.

Let's do the right thing, pick up this book today, and let me show you how to work smarter, not harder. You can transform your Real Estate career into something you and your family will be proud of for years to come.

I'm looking forward to working with you on the other side!

Reset your Mindset

Okay, everyone, I want you to understand this, so I need you to get comfortable. Turn off Facebook and Twitter. Find a part in your home or office where you can relax and not be disturbed.

Now open your mind to the possibilities of increasing your business.

The first thing that we need to do is reset our thinking and our beliefs because if you don't believe in yourself, how in the hell is someone going to trust you with their most important asset? There's a reason that we're on this God-given Earth. Each one of us has our own purpose in life. Some of us know what it is, and some of us do not, but most of us will never know.

If you're reading this book, you can take control of this moment and find out what your strength is, what your weaknesses are, and turn them both around to your advantage.

We're coming close to the home stretch of the end of the year, and this is no time to take your foot off the pedal. No matter how good or bad your year was up to this point, right now you must change your future.

Real Estate is the only business I know where you can make as much money as you want, and all you have to do is help as many people as you can. We get paid more than doctors, lawyers, or even brain surgeons. All we have to do for a very comfortable lifestyle is prospect three hours a day, five days a week.

Look deep down inside yourself, and ask: what motivates me?
Family, cars, money, or maybe it's just making ends meet? I can tell you from personal experience, worrying about your finances will drive you crazy, keep you up at night, and if you're not careful, kill you. That's why it's more important than ever to watch what you think and feel, or who you interact with, because this will affect you in more ways than you can realize.

Energy Suckers

If you're hanging around someone that's always complaining, nagging or downright depressing, you must cut them off. They are sucking the life force out of you. I love this quote from Oprah Winfrey:

"You know this to be true. There are some energy suckers in your life. Just literally, taking the life force out of you. You will never be able to do or be who you supposed to be in the world as long as you continue to buy into the energy suckers."

Guard your positive energy, your positive mindset, and your well-being as if your life depends on it because actually, it does. Your whole future in Real Estate depends on your mindset. If you claim your doubt, insecurities, and imperfections, they're going to become apparent to other people. If you claim to yourself, I am confident, I'm knowledgeable, and I'm going to do the best work possible, that also will show through to your colleagues, clients, and your family.

Keep Life Simple!

The first thing we need to do is just keep life simple. It might be easier said than done, but let go and let God. Most of the things we stress over can be easily resolved if we just let it go. For example, say you're driving down the street and someone cuts you off. You're hollering and screaming at them, your blood pressure is going up, your eyes turn red, your face fills up with anger, and for what? They don't even realize what they've done, and they don't even notice that you're upset.

So, for the rest of the day you carry this anger with you in some form or fashion. Did you know by continuously being stressed out, worried or angry, you are speeding up the aging process 2.7%? I'm sure no one wants to get old before their time.

If I need to calm down, relax, or reset my emotional clock, I have this relaxation technique I use. The cool thing about this technique is it works well for people that suffer from panic attacks, anxiety, or in any situation where you need calm down.

When you feel yourself getting angry or super anxious, this is the best time to start this technique.

1. Take a deep breath through your mouth and fill your lungs up with air, as much as possible, and hold it.
2. At the same time you're holding your breath, you need to tense up all your muscles all over your body from your toes, legs, midsection, neck, and your face. Tense everything for five to ten seconds and hold.
3. After the five to ten seconds are up, relax and let the air out of your body steadily.

I know you're probably saying to yourself, "This Real Estate guy is crazy."

I thought so too when it was first introduced to me, but after I did it, I was amazed by the wave of tension, stress, and fear that just left my body immediately.

Like anything it takes practice, and when I first started doing it, sometimes I would have to do it two or three times to get the full effect. As time went on, certain things did not trigger my anger or my anxiety anymore.

Just changing your mindset and your thinking toward certain things, and getting in the habit of letting things go will take time, even with the help of this technique, but trust me, you will feel better in the long term.

Your Morning Routine

What type of morning routine do you have? Did you know most people wake up just early enough to get ready and go to work? That's barely enough time wash up, brush your teeth, have a decent bathroom run, change into your clothes, and run out the door. This throws off your day because you're always playing catch up.

I've been in transportation for over twenty years and I know the highest probable time to have a car accident is before 9 a.m. and after 5 p.m., Monday through Friday, excluding holidays.

That's a different beast altogether. Most of the accidents in the morning are because people are running late and they are trying to shave off time. They're cutting you off, running lights, and driving recklessly. I'm sure you noticed it.

Do this: change your morning routine.

Why don't you wake up an hour, NO, two hours early, every morning? It's like you have a head start on the world. Yeah, it's going to take some getting used to, but you'll notice right off the bat how things look new and different when you wake up a little early. You don't feel so rushed, you can relax, pray, meditate, or read a good book. When you're driving to the office, you notice the lighter traffic. People are not in such a rush, and it sets the pace for your day. Wake up a few minutes earlier every day, and let me know how it works for you.

Exercise

Okay let's talk about exercise! Exercise is the number one way to make you feel better. Yes, I know, sometimes it's hard. You feel sad, depressed lethargic, lazy, and the list goes on and on. Let's face it, you don't have to be a scientist to know exercise is good for you. It keeps your weight in check, and makes you physically fit and stronger. Working out keeps you feeling youthful and active, and keeps obesity and its diseases at bay. With continuous exercise, you can most likely live a nice active life into old age.

Another advantage I love about exercise is it helps you with your mindset by improving the way you feel. Exercise actually makes you a happier person, and relieves your stress. I don't know the technical jargon. Let's just say it releases happy chemicals into your brain.

This helps you with anxiety and stress. My personal example comes from when I was going through a tough time during my divorce. I noticed myself working out more. I found myself less stressed after a workout. I was able to think clearly and make better decisions.

When you exercise, it stresses your body at a low level by raising your breathing, heart rate, and exhausting your muscles to a certain extent. Of course, it depends on which exercises you do and how long the session lasts. With continuous exercise, you will eventually condition your whole body and mind to better handle life's stresses. Less stress equals a better quality of life!

I'm just going to put it out there: I'm insecure about how I look, and I know I'm not the only one. When you exercise and eat right, that weight starts slowly burning off. Yes, it's hard work, but when you start seeing the scale reading lower numbers, that boosts your self-confidence, makes you feel better, and makes you want to work harder to reach your goals.

If you purchased this book, most likely we're in the same industry: Real Estate! You can relate to my crazy mixed-up world that's never the same from one day to the next. I'm going to give you three tips to make it easier for you to put that Sweat Equity in getting your body, mind, and soul in shape:

1. **Schedule your workouts** - As a successful Real Estate Agent, you should be scheduling everything: prospecting, appointments, and workouts should be no different. Once you actively put it in your schedule, you won't be able to miss it. It's locked in. Set the dates, time, duration, and what type of workout it will be, so when it pops up on your calendar, you're

prepared.

I know different agents work out at different times during the day. I personally love working out in the morning before the sun comes up. There is just something about a brand-new morning and having that brand-new feeling of life.
2. **Workout posse or friends** - It's always better to work out with friends, so talk to other Agents in your office, friends, or relatives. Work on that support network, so that way you'll have a higher level of staying power through accountability. When you're working out with friends or a group, there is just something about the energy of others that helps your self-esteem to build you up and increase your motivation.
3. **Just do it** - I love those Nike commercials. Just do it! Find your greatness. If you don't know what I'm talking about, just go on YouTube and do a search. You will be inspired. To move ahead in this world, you must take action, so no more excuses or putting it off.

The best way to be prepared for your exercise is to have your clothes ready the night before. Whenever you work out, have a workout bag with a change of clothes. That way when you're ready to hit the gym, you're all set.

Having a good playlist to listen to can be a motivator as well. If you would like to see what I use or where I work out, just check out my YouTube channel: https://www.youtube.com/channel/UCXxXrnEm4jxa_TtDs73Xjuw (Search "willie j may enterprises" on YouTube).

Hopefully this will motivate you to act, and once you do, you will feel much better about yourself, your health, and about your future.

Hot Lead Sources

There's countless lead sources out there for a Real Estate Agent to choose from. There's no time to be distracted. We need to hyper focus our lead generation efforts to generate business now and narrow our focus on certain lead sources that will generate a high probability of success.

It's like we're a sniper zeroing in on our target unlike most agents who are using the shotgun technique praying they will hit something. We have a goal in mind: target immediate and continuous business.

We're going to focus our prospecting efforts on:

- Expired Listings
- For Sale By Owners
- FSBO Open Houses
- Past clients
- SOI/Databases

For this system, we are mainly looking for listings rather than working with buyers. If you run across a buyer that is motivated, meaning a buyer who is going to follow your instructions and has a definite time frame on purchasing a home, then definitely work with that buyer. If not, refer that buyer out for a referral fee.

Expired Listings

The always popular Expired Listings. Expired Listings are the number one source of immediate business for any Real Estate Agent. They've been on the market for over six months and haven't sold. There could be several reasons why the home didn't sell: bad location, substandard condition, falling apart, no showings, no lock box for easy accessibility, and the number one reason, the property is overpriced.

One of the good things about Expired Listings is that a highly successful Real Estate Agent will lay the foundation and inform the sellers about what is needed to sell a house in their market. In most cases, those listings will not expire.

What works in our favor is most Expired Listings are expired because the Agent wasn't strong enough to inform their client about what needs to be done to get their property sold for top dollar. As a result, the property expires, and the clients are upset because they wasted six months of their lives just to be that much farther away from their goals and dreams of moving on with their lives.

Our job is getting in front of the Expired Listing and letting them know that we're the authority on getting their home sold for top dollar. If they are still motivated to move, then we should do whatever we can to stay in front of them. When the time is right, we get hired and do what is necessary to get their property sold and have happy clients.

For Sale by Owners

These are the DIY people who love doing everything on their own. After it doesn't work, they call a professional to clean it up. FSBOs are just regular people like you and me that are either trying to do it on their own just to see if they can, or they are trying to save some cash just as you or I would on any expensive purchase.

When you go to a car lot, you know you are going to have to haggle, so you try to do your homework because you know it's going to be a fight when you talk to the salesman. If you aren't careful, you will be driving off into the sunset with buyer's remorse.

As Real Estate Agents, we already don't have the most pristine reputation. Be mindful when you interact with potential clients. Always be professional, courteous, and let them know without a shadow of a doubt that you know exactly how to get their home sold.

FSBO Open Houses

Say what? For Sale By Owner Open Houses! I understand a lot of Agents haven't heard of this practice or are unwilling to utilize this technique, but our main purpose is to jump start our business. What better way to jump start our business than work with FSBO's looking to sell now.

By providing the FSBO with helpful information on how to sell the property by themselves, after a while they'll realize it's not as easy as it seems to sell a house. By offering them help on an extra level with Open Houses, you put yourself in the position where you can possibly double the transaction, or at the bare minimum, get some good leads on some buyers looking to buy right now. So, For Sale By Owner Open Houses work very well as a shot of adrenaline to your Real Estate business.

Sphere of Influence (SOI)/Database

Your sphere of influence or your database consists of:

- Friends
- Family
- Acquaintances
- Past clients
- Current clients
- Neighbors

The list goes on and on. The short definition is, **Everyone You Know.** Let's think about this for a minute. It's not only everyone you know, it's everyone you know that knows you sell Real Estate.

Ask yourself: of all the people you know, how many of them know you sell Real Estate?

If you're thinking to yourself, "Hmmm…not so many", then it looks like we have some work to do.

Taking Massive Action

"The graveyard is the richest place on earth, because it is here that you will find all the hopes and dreams that were never fulfilled, the books that were never written, the songs that were never sung, the inventions that were never shared, the cures that were never discovered, all because someone was too afraid to take that first step, keep with the problem, or determined to carry out their dream."
- Les Brown

How bad do you want to be successful? Are you willing to put in the effort for what it takes to be a successful Realtor? If you really consider the lives of successful individuals throughout history, you'll see they invested a massive amount of time building their business. We all know success does not come overnight. One of the best advantages that we have in the Real Estate industry is that success can be duplicated.

Let me say this again just in case you didn't catch it the first time: **success can be duplicated**.

If you have the directions to the destination, you will succeed. Now following those directions may be a problem. Life might get in the way, self-doubt, lack of motivation, any number of things might get in the way. That's why I asked you how bad do you want to be successful. The thing is if you want it bad enough, you'll make it happen. I believe in you and I know you can be successful. All you have to do, is invest in yourself with some old fashioned hard work.

Focus on the Basics

Avoidance behavior, scared to get started, self-doubt, not knowing what to say, not having the courage to push through...understand that we all go through these emotions when we are new. Sometimes when we are seasoned veterans, these insecurities may creep back in because we're complacent about our business.

We don't have to have the greatest mind on the planet to succeed in Real Estate. Just be consistent! By turning your attention to, and focusing on the basics, you will be able to build a successful foundation in Real Estate.

Let me tell you how...

One of the main characteristics of a successful agent is communication, right? You and I can agree most us are not born as exceptional communicators. What this means is that good communication, or having any good dialogue with your client must be learned, practiced, and rehearsed, so you can get good, great, and eventually reach the point of mastery.

For you to close more deals for the holidays or any other time for that matter, you have to be prepared for the opportunities. In the beginning of my career, I lost many transactions because I did not know the proper words to say. I just did not have the experience that was needed to lock down the listing.

It happened to me, it will happen to you. It's just part of the learning process. I guess you could say it's like on-the-job training because every situation and transaction are different. If a situation or transaction knocks you flat on your back, learn from that, get up, dust yourself off, and move on to the next deal. Your mistakes, your situations, your customers, and all the learning experience that you face in business and in life will make you a better Real Estate Agent for yourself and for your customers. When you make a mistake, do not beat yourself up. Learn from it and move on. You'll be a better agent as a result.

I would suggest working on your scripts in the morning just before you hit the phones and before any other prospecting activity. If you're new in the business, I would suggest practicing/role-playing for forty-five minutes to an hour every day before each session.

If you've been a Real Estate Agent for a while and you're familiar with your scripts, I still suggest you practice for at least fifteen to thirty minutes before each prospecting session. I don't know how many times I knew what to say, but for some reason, my mind went blank for that split-second and the client hung up on me. Consistently practicing your scripts is mastering the basics.

The more you practice the better you become. Practicing with different role play partners will build up your confidence and your stamina for prospecting.

If you're scared of calling or you have call reluctance, try out this schedule for a twelve-hour call session:

Call from 8:00 a.m. until 8:00 p.m. Have two breaks of ten minutes each in the morning. Take an hour for lunch. Take two more ten-minute breaks before 5 p.m. Take a forty-five-minute break, and finish out your session at 8:00 p.m.

I will guarantee you that you'll be completely physically and mentally exhausted from cold calling, but this is like getting tried by fire. This is well worth the education that you will learn by doing a marathon session.

In this twelve-hour session you probably made more contacts and dials then most agents do in their first years in the business. On top of that great feat, you now have more confidence and determination to be successful. Now with this newly developed confidence, you can talk to anybody. You will soon see your business go to the next level.

Top 10 Reasons Why You Should Sell During the Holidays

You're going to come across a lot of sellers not wanting to sell for whatever reason. If they have a strong motivation to move, it's your job to guide them to their dreams and goals. Most likely they just have cold feet. They want to be 100% confident they're making the right decision. Remember, this is the most expensive transaction most people make in their entire lifetime.

To ensure your success in speaking to your clients regarding selling their homes for the holidays, I've devised ten reasons why you should sell during the holidays. This is like a cheat sheet to counter their responses. Knowing how to overcome these objections should boost your confidence and drive you to take massive action to get in front of your clients.

In my experience these ten reasons will help you secure the listing and move forward with putting their property on the market for a successful closing.

1. When you have your house up for sale during the holidays, we can schedule showings around your life. This way, you will not be disturbed on certain days you wish not to have your property available.
2. 80% of new job transfers start in January of a new year. Buyers that are affected with the transfer are highly motivated to purchase now.
3. Taxes are coming up at the end of each year, so some people have to purchase just because of tax reasons.
4. By selling your home during the holidays, you can buy your new house in Spring when there are more houses on the market. With more homes on the market, prices are lower with more competition. This allows you to come into the Spring market as a non-contingent buyer. This helps streamline the process of purchasing your new home.

5. Buyers have more time during the holidays to search for their new home. More days off and extended weekends are a great opportunity to get your property sold to these highly motivated buyers.
6. Buyers are highly motivated & emotional. They are mentally in the holiday season. They're looking to buy now! So, they will be more motivated to pay your price.
7. During the holidays, your competition is taking their property off the market to relist in the new year with everyone else. In the meantime, the current buyers have less properties to choose from. Every year this activates the law of Real Estate: **supply and demand**. When supplies go down, you have a greater opportunity to get more money for your property.
8. When you have your home decorated for the holidays, your home will show better. There is nothing like a buyer falling in love with your home and submitting a full-price offer!
9. If a buyer is looking to purchase a property during the holidays, this means they're a very motivated buyer for whatever reason. If they're motivated, the transaction is quicker and much smoother because they're highly motivated to close quickly. The truth is: holiday buyers are more serious buyers!

10. And the TOP reason why you should sell your home during the holidays is: my brokerage and I have sold over 500 homes this year. With our proven sales model we can sell your home for top dollar. More important than that, you stated to me that you wanted to be sold and moved before the first of the year. We can do that for you!

GOLDEN NUGGET: Always use your sales stats. If not yours, then the stats of your company. You can also use the surrounding neighborhood sales stats as well. Remind them of their motivation to sell, and that you have a proven system to get the job done.

The Holiday Game Plan

Okay, all you hungry Real Estate Agents out there, it's time to kick our business into high gear. Like I mentioned earlier, we're going to go into a select few lead generation sources to maximize our potential for obtaining listings, and getting them closed as soon as possible.

There are just a few more things to cover before we get into the game plan. Fourth Quarter is usually one of the best times out of the year to prospect. Yeah, yeah, you're going to get a lot of people saying, "Oh we're not going to sell during the holidays", "nobody buys during the holidays", "we have friends and family coming over for the holidays", etc.

Homeowners don't like to be disturbed over the holidays.

You could make up as many excuses as you want not to go after a prospect during the holidays, but the fact remains, no matter what time of year it is, you're going to have people needing to buy and sell Real Estate. Log into your own MLS and check the stats as far back as you can and look at how many properties have come on the market in the last Fourth Quarter. How many properties sold in December?

I'm telling you this, so you can understand, open your eyes, and see without a shadow of a doubt that even in a low-inventory market, you have listings that will hit the market every day. There is no excuse not to prospect and go after those potential clients that need your help to sell. So, let's get started!

Expired Listings

Nothing gets me more excited than receiving highly motivated leads each morning when I log into my computer. First off, I'm if you have a contact management system, that you're using to retrieve your leads and store them. If you would like recommendations, you can check out my book *Top 10 Expired Objections* - http://amzn.to/2zdYnYY.

I understand that if you've been in the business for a while you're set on your own style of prospecting. However, if you're new in the business, you probably do not have a clue where to begin. No problem, I have your back.

What we're going to do is set a small goal. In this way, you can achieve that goal and be successful. No matter when you start your commitment for prospecting, you must have a made-up mind and a commitment to 10X your prospecting for thirty days. Thirty days is not that long and not that short.

Look at it like this: the small steps you make every day transform into the compound effect. It will build up over time. Each day you do money-making activities is a higher chance that you get rewarded in the future. Each day counts and each contact counts.

Do not take your relationship for granted. That is future potential income.

Working with Expired Listings, you must make sure that you have a game plan including a contact method with which you're comfortable. My contact method of choice is the telephone, but there are other contact methods as well. This is my list in order of effectiveness:

- Door knocking
- Phone calls
- Direct Mail

Expired Door Knocking

Door knocking is one of the most effective ways to go after an Expired Listing. The reason is that there are not that many highly-motivated Real Estate Agents going after Expired Listings on a 10x scale, much less picking up the phone and calling.

I said it before, and I'll say it again: **belly to belly, face to face**.

It's the number one best method of prospecting.

When you talk to the Expired Listing, most likely they're going to be impressed that you are taking the extra steps to offer your services to help them and their family move forward.

When you go to the Expired door, make sure you're prepared with a pre-list package or some sort of tri-fold brochure that has your information on it, how you do business, and your testimonials to give to the potential client. This next part is very important: make sure that the information you're giving them is on high-quality paper because remember, you're a higher-class Agent! You must demonstrate it accordingly.

If you're new to the business and you do not have promotional material for yourself, I would suggest that you have your brokerage, or a fellow agent help you. If you do not have past clients, fall back on the satisfied clients of your brokerage. Ask your broker if it's okay to use some of the company's satisfied clients as testimonials.

When you go out door-to-door for Expired Listings, one the many things you want to look for is if there are absentee owners or is the property owner-occupied? You need to know which one is which. You don't want to be pulling up to an Expired Listing and knocking on the door to a renter at seven or eight in the morning. That's not going to be a very good experience at all.

Make sure you do your homework. An absentee owner is a homeowner that owns the property but lives in a different location. An owner-occupied property is when the homeowner actually lives in the home. Our strategy is to go after both, but we do it the correct way. When you identify the absentee owner, make a note of the property that has Expired and the current resident. With an owner-occupied property, you know you can contact the seller directly by going straight to the property.

Another thing I would suggest when you're knocking on those Expired doors is to always be prepared. Always have a few blank copies of the listing agreement with you. You won't get the listing every time, but you always want to be prepared. If the opportunity presents itself, take the listing right then and there. It will happen. You must be prepared for it.

Expired Door Knocking Script:

Script for when you're at the Expired Listing door:

> My name is William with Super Agent Realty. Good morning Mr. Seller.

Seller: Good morning.

My report shows your home was for sale, but somehow left the market unsold. Is this correct?

Seller: Yes.

I'm sorry to hear that. There's been six homes in the area that sold while your home was on the market, so we know that homes are selling. If you were able to get your price and be under contract in the next two to three weeks, would that be of interest to you?

Seller: Yes.

Great I can definitely sell your house. Let's do this I'm going to go to the office, do my homework on your property, and come back today at 3 p.m. Will you be home?

This is not being pushy this is being in authority, and sure of yourself. This demonstrates your professionalism. You're demonstrating that you can sell their house. People respect that.

Seller: Yes.

If the seller says no but has another time, make yourself available for that time to take the listing.

> Great, what's your best email address?
>
> This way I can send you some information about me, my company, and how I sell homes differently than other Agents. I'll also bring my real and accurate past client testimonials.

If this is a brand-new Expired, let them know they're going to be bombarded with phone calls from other Agents looking to take the listing. Always remember your main goal when contacting Expireds is setting the appointment. Once you have the appointment set for your return and the email address, then ask the pre-qualification questions if the conversation permits:

- Where are you moving to?
- How soon do you want to have this home sold by?
- Realistically, how much would you like to sell the house for?
- What do you think caused your home not to sell?

You can probably ask a million more pre-qualification questions, but we want to keep the interaction short, brief, and to the point when we are door knocking.

Understand that door knocking is very effective, but also very time-consuming. After you make contact, decide on the status of the contact. What I mean is discerning if the contact is worth following up or if it's just trash. The quicker you can categorize the prospect, the quicker you can move on to the next property.

DOOR KNOCKING BONUS TIP: If you want to 10x your door knocking efforts and obtain a few more listings for the holidays, prospect old Expireds; Expireds going back six, eight, or twenty-four months back. When you siphon through them, separate the good from the bad, the sold from the unsold, and ones with numbers from ones without.

For the ones without numbers that are not listed, those are the perfect prospects to go to the door, and show them your USP or Unique Selling Proposition that should be included in your well-built, pre-list package.

Most of the time, the Expired Listing is not current on the recent Market activity. When they expired, they were overpriced or there was some other reason that caused them to expire. If it's been a few months or even a few years since they've been on the market, their home has most likely gained equity and the value has increased. You can show them that being sold at that price is more of a reality now.

Calling the Expired Listings

To catch the new Expired, you must be one of the first agents to contact them in the morning. Make it a ritual to be in your office or your home office ready to make calls no later than 7:45 a.m. I learned a long time ago that when you're the first person to give them a call, you have an 80% better chance on setting the appointment if they are still motivated to sell. If you're not one of the first ones to contact the Expireds, your percentage goes way down.

In my experience, contacting Expireds and having an actual, beneficial, positive, friendly, conversation most often occurs between 7:45 and 8:30 a.m. After that, all hell breaks loose. Why? Because while you're having a conversation with the Expired Listing, you notice other people are calling while you're trying to have that conversation. You definitely know who's calling at 8:00 a.m., right? Yes! It's your competition!

Usually by 8:30 or 9:00 a.m., they are fed up. Their phones have been ringing off the hook constantly. At this point, they either take the phone off the hook, turn off their ringer, or just simply don't answer. If they do answer, prepare to be cussed out and called all sorts of names that are not on your birth certificate. We, as Agents, understand why they're upset. They had their house on the market, and for whatever reason, it did not sell.

Suddenly, out of the blue, we're calling them trying to take the listing. In their minds it does not make any sense. They are thinking, "Where were all these agents when I had my house on the market before?"

To understand the seriousness of this, let me tell you this story:

I was already in my second hour of prospecting on a Saturday morning. It was the first day of the month and everyone knows or should know, if the first day of the month falls on a weekend, that's the very best day to prospect Expired Listings. You have less competition because it's the weekend, and you have a higher contact rate. More people are off during the weekend, so it's a win-win. You still have competition but not as much.

Back to the story: I was making my calls and it sounded like an older lady answering the phone. It also sounded like her voice was cracking. What became apparent moments into my script was that she was trying to communicate, but her crying was getting in the way of her trying to speak to me.

The woman was crying and highly stressed. She could barely communicate at all during the first few minutes or so of the call. After I realized she was crying, I tried my best to console her by asking what was wrong and if there was anything I could do.

After she was able to calm down a little bit, she said, "I wish you damn Agents would stop calling me and leave me the hell alone. The house is not for sale, so don't call me anymore."

Right after she made her statement she promptly hung up on me. I did not hesitate and dialed her right back. Surprisingly she answered, and before she could cuss me out or fuss at me, I said, "Ma'am, ma'am, I know you're going through a tough time right now, I just want to know what's going on to see how I can help."

She replied with a stoner tone and said, "Can you bring my husband back from the dead?"

That took me by surprise. I was silent.
"Of course not." she said.

After I gained my composure, I said, "I need to take a break from work right now, and it seems like you need someone to talk to. I have thirty minutes or so if you would like to talk and tell me what's going on. Maybe afterward, we can see if I can help you or not. If not, at least you have someone to talk to for a few minutes, and you're able to avoid all those callers harassing you. What do you say...I'm all yours."

She began to talk and told me how her husband died of a stroke a few months earlier and how hard it had been on her and her family. They were married for over forty years, and now with him gone, it was just her and the mortgage.

The only way to preserve the equity they built together in the house was to sell it. For forty years, her husband handled all the finances. Since he's been gone, she has fallen behind on the mortgage. Since the property didn't sell, she is in danger of foreclosure. She had no one to help or guide her, and the previous Agent just slapped the property on the market with an overpriced price tag. Of course, it expired.

After talking with her about an hour and half, she became more relaxed and open-minded. I was completely honest, and I told her I understood what she was going through. I told her that I wasn't sure I could help, but the first thing I could do was come look at her house and tell her exactly why it hadn't sold. I planned to share my proven plan to get her home listed and sold. I let her know that it wouldn't cost her anything, it would only take a few minutes, and that this wasn't my first rodeo.

I met her at the house later that day and I told her that in the condition it was in, it was not surprising her home did not sell. However, I was pretty sure with a few changes, we could sell the house faster and for more money than before.

Long story short, I had someone come cut her grass and clean up the backyard. We painted the outside of the house as well as the inside. After everything was complete, I relisted the property with a detailed description and at least forty professional pictures. Within twenty-four hours we received multiple offers and the property sold $6,000 over list price. I also added another raving fan to my database.

I'm telling you this story because it doesn't matter if you're new in the business, or if you have little to no experience. You have your brokerage and your fellow

Agents that support you. Maybe you have been in the business for a while, and you're nervous about calling Expireds. You need to understand we're here to help people. In the story, I took the extra steps to help somebody in need. Don't chase after the mighty dollar.

> *"You will get all you want in life, if you help enough other people get what they want."* -Zig Ziglar

You probably hear this all the time, and I know I've said it a few times: prospecting is a numbers game. You must call quite a few Expireds to get through to the golden nuggets. That's why they call it prospecting.

Expired Calling Script:

>My name is William with Super Agent Realty. Good morning Mr. Seller.
>
>**Seller:** Good morning.
>
>My report shows your home was for sale, but somehow left the market unsold. Is this correct?
>
>**Seller:** Yes.

For the right price, are you still interested in selling?

Seller: Yes.

I specialize in helping homeowners that were on the market, but didn't sell for whatever reason. I would love to see how I can help. I'm available today at 5 or would 6:30 be better for your schedule?

Seller: 6 p.m.

Sounds great, what is your best email address? I would like to send you information about me, my company, and how I do business differently than other Agents. Also, you can read the testimonials of my past clients.

After you get the email, move forward to the pre-qualification questions.

Keep the conversation short, sweet, and to the point. At the same time, try to build rapport by letting them talk 80% of the time while you talk 20% of the time with questions.

Direct Mail Campaigns

The advantage of direct mail is that you can contact the homeowner if they don't live in the area or reside out-of-state. Send them a letter letting them know that you're the neighborhood expert, and then send out a newsletter once a month with updates on current sales in their area.

You can mail different materials from newsletters to postcards to magazines. It's amazing how creative you can be with direct mail. Be careful because postage can get expensive.

Like any other form of prospecting, direct mail is a numbers game. If you run a direct mail campaign during the holidays, you run the risk of getting lost in the shuffle.

In my experience, Agents who don't prospect door-to-door or via telephone usually lean on direct mail. Several times, I've arrived at an appointment with an Expired Listing to find a mountain of mail from other Agents all over the counter soliciting for their business.

My advice is if you decide to use direct mail as a part of your Expired prospecting, that you do so in conjunction with door knocking and cold calling. You can't build a rapport with a potential client through the mail. You must establish a connection. Take the time to write a thank you note after you speak with them. Many times, I receive a call saying thanks for the card, and that makes me feel good. I want to work that much harder.

It's not often we get thank you cards anymore. Everything is email or instant messenger. Sometimes snail mail still brings a smile to someone's face. In most cases, my experience is that it solidifies the business relationship.

I also use Send Out Cards. I love Send Out Cards because you can customize the card whatever way you like. I will take a picture of the property and have a sold banner across it. I send it to the client, and let them know this can be them in the future.

Expired Follow-Up:

Did you know 80% of Real Estate Agents do not follow up on their leads? If you are spending all your time hunting down the prospect, having a good conversation with them, building rapport, and you don't follow up, you're wasting your damn time. You've probably heard this before, but I will say it again, so you can get it ingrained in your brain because you *must* understand this to be successful: **the money is in the follow-up!**

Yes, we're on the subject of expired follow-up, but follow-up needs to be done in all forms of prospecting including cold calling, Expireds, For Sale By Owners, SOI, & your beloved database.

You must exercise frequent, consistent, continuous, persistent follow-up. Each time you follow up, you build layers upon layers of rapport, and with that, TRUST. Depending on your market, it takes anywhere from eight to fifteen contacts for you to set an appointment just so you have the opportunity to present. Do you know your competition will contact Expireds one or two times, maybe even three times on a good day?

The good thing about being in Quarter Four is that most of your competition will be taking off on vacation, slacking off, or just quit the business until the first of the year. As I mentioned earlier in the book, every day you have new listings in your market. When you have less competition that increases your likelihood to acquire more listings. If you don't put in the work necessary to follow up on these Expired gems, the top-producing agents in your market know the value of follow-up. When you don't follow up, it's like giving your money away to them. So, do the follow-up work that needs to be done, and get yourself on their radar.

The Expired Follow-Up System

My expired follow-up system is simple. The first thing I do is kick call reluctance to the curb because there's no space for me not to make my calls. I need to support my family and I'm working very hard to achieve my financial dreams. Knowing that each time I have a closing in my market, I receive a commission anywhere from $10,000-$15,000 puts fire into my prospecting.

Number One - I make my initial call to the Expired prospect. I am looking to have a beneficial conversation with nice, sane individuals that may even ask for a call back. Before I let them go, I make sure to secure an email address. I'd say 40% of the time with a new Expired you can retrieve the email.

If I do retrieve the email, I put them in my system to receive a monthly snapshot of homes that sold in their area. Also, I will send them a custom template email introducing myself. Finally, I print this and other contacts out during my prospecting, so at the end of my prospecting session I can go back to that stack. I send each one a personalized thank you card.

Basically, I say:

> Hello Mr./Mrs. Homeowner,
>
> It was a pleasure speaking with you the other day. You have a wonderful home and I know it will sell quickly. You mentioned you were frustrated with the process. I completely understand. No rush. If you ever need me, I have enclosed my business card. Have a great day.
>
> Sincerely,
> William

I don't write anything fancy. I just put in the card what I'm feeling, and I suggest you do the same. You certainly don't have to use my words, but you can use them as a foundation. Remember, they are getting bombarded with Agents calling and sending letters, so make sure you mention your conversation in the card. It will help them remember you.

Number Two - I normally have things set up to call them again in five or six days. This gives my card plenty of time to arrive. If it's a new Expired, that will hopefully give things time to calm down as far as other Agents calling as well.

Example of my call when I don't have their email:

> Mr. Seller, this is William with Super Agent Realty, good morning.
>
> **Seller:** Good morning. How can I help you?
>
> I was just giving you a quick follow-up call. We spoke a few days ago, and you mentioned to me that you're taking your property off the market and not interested in selling any longer. Is that still the case?
>
> **Seller:** Yes.
>
> Okay, I can understand that. Did you know in the last three weeks fourteen homes sold, and nine of those homes sold over asking price? Would you like me to send you the information?
>
> **Seller:** Yes, I would, thank you.
>
> What is your best email address, so I can get that over to you right away?
>
> **Seller:** hotseller@gmail.com
>
> Okay, thank you. I'll get that over to you right away. In the meantime, I would like to set up a

time where I could come over and look at your house. I can show you exactly why it didn't sell and what it takes to get it sold in this market. I'm available today at 5 or would 6:30 be better for your schedule?

Seller: Not now, maybe later.

Okay, I completely understand. I'm just curious were you able to receive my information?

Seller: Oh yes, your thank you card. Thank you!

That's great. Now that I know you have my information, when would be a good time for me to check back in with you?

Seller: Give me two months.

No problem. I'll put it in my calendar, and make sure I stay in touch. Thank you for your time and have a great day.

As you can see, I'm not too pushy about setting the appointment. I'm all about building the relationship, trust, and rapport over time. If I'm not pushy, they will gradually and naturally build some sort of bond with me. In most cases after the transaction, I have more than just a satisfied customer, I have a friend for life. And may I add -- **a Raving Fan!**

In this example, I showed an example of my follow-up script along with asking for the email. Now since I have the email, I will put it into my system, and confirm they received my email the following day.

Also in this example, he instructed me to give him a call in two months. Generally, you cut that in half; however, if the market has a low inventory, I would stay right on top of them. For example, I would send a card with a picture of their house with a sold banner on the front. Inside, put a screen shot of the neighborhood sales on one side and the ones that sold highest. Three or four properties are enough. On the other side, let them know you just wanted to give them an update and remind them that their home will sell quickly.

If I'm going over your head regarding Send Out Cards and how they work, check out my YouTube video here - http://williejmayenterprises.com/Send_Out_Cards. You can also see more on my website - http://williejmayenterprises.com/recommendations-from-william/

Number Three - After I make the initial steps previously mentioned, I set the potential clients up in my contact management system to receive an automatic call back every other month. I use the same script each time:

> Mr. Seller this is William with Super Agent Realty, good morning.
>
> I was just giving you a quick follow-up call. We spoke a while back and you mentioned to me that you're _____. Is that still the case?
>
> Okay, I can understand that. Did you know in the last _____, there were _____ homes that sold, and _____ of those homes sold over asking price? Were you aware that the market is that active?
>
> I would like to pop by, and go over three things that will definitely affect the money you put in your pocket when you decide to sell.
>
> First, I would like to look at your home and see what you have to offer the buyers in today's market.

Second, I want to show you a few things that will draw in qualified buyers interested in paying top dollar for your home.

Mr. Seller, would you say that's pretty important for your bottom line?

Seller: Yes!

The third thing is, I'm going to show you why my homes sell, and other Agents' homes do not in this market.

We can get together today at 5 or would 6:30 tomorrow be better for your schedule?

That's it. There's nothing to it. Well, maybe there's a lot to it. You must keep on following up and gauge their motivation. Update the contact record each time you make a contact. Even if they say they're no longer selling, continue to follow up unless they tell you not to. When you follow up, use the FORD technique:

- Family
- Occupation
- Recreation
- Dreams

I will go into more detail on this in a later chapter.

At the end of the conversation, ask for referrals. You know what to say, right?

> Who do you know that is looking to buy or sell Real Estate now or in the near future?

As you get more comfortable on the phone, your follow-up and interactions with prospects will improve and increase. Once you get over the initial hurdle of it being uncomfortable, you'll soon start developing a habit of being on the phones interacting with clients and closing deals.

I can just see you now in a few short months taking the steps you've learned from this book to increase your business tenfold. All of it simply because you put forth the work and you embraced the truth: **the money is in the follow-up**.

Just a reminder if you're having trouble with expired objections, check out my other book *Top 10 Expired Objections*. Get a link to it on Amazon from my website - http://williejmayenterprises.com/

For Sale By Owners

I just love Real Estate. You have the Expired Listing that, for whatever reason, expired. You're jumping up and down saying "thank you" to the Real Estate gods for giving you such a great source of business. The icing on the cake is For Sale By Owner or FSBO. These people are the DIY generation who want to do it themselves. They say, "I can save myself the commission. Who needs a Real Estate Agent!?!"

They think it's easy until they try to do it themselves, and then they realize, they need us.

Always remember we are professionals and we should act accordingly. If an FSBO or anyone for that matter, doesn't appreciate your value, move on. There will always be more leads, so don't get stuck on just one client. Have an abundance mindset. To be good at working with Expireds and FSBOs, we have to determine their motivation and if that person is someone with which we are comfortable working.

A lot of Agents try to sell the FSBO on how they cannot sell their house on their own. The truth is they can sell on their own. The real question is: do they want to sell on their own just to see if they can do it, or do they want to sell their home for the most money possible? As a top-producing Real Estate Agent, this is what you need to find out before you go any further.

Identifying the Three Types of FSBOs

FSBOs fall into three categories. (This technique also works for Expireds.) When you reach out to them, it's your job to find out which category fits them best.

1. **Ready and willing to meet** - This group is willing to hear what you have to say and sets an appointment with you.
2. **Not ready; still trying to sell on their own** - These prospects need more time to try to sell on their own. Sooner or later, they will realize doing things on their own is not what it's cracked up to be. With continuous follow-up and persistence, you will have a higher level of conversions than your competition who never follow up.
3. **Trash** - These prospects are not worth following up with. You will encounter a lot of prospects that you have to eliminate for different reasons. For example, a seller who has no or very little equity to pay commission is out. Other examples include, another Agent

selling an off-market listing, or an investor who isn't willing to cooperate with Agents.

Anytime you are telephone prospecting, the main goal is trying to set an appointment. At first, you will be nervous, unsure of yourself, and doubtful of your abilities. If you practice role playing and rehearse, you will see your skills get better. The more FSBOs you call, you will see your confidence grow. If I am rusty, say after a vacation or long weekend, I just call without caring what happens during the conversation to get back in verbal shape. You will be pleasantly surprised sometimes to get listings this way.

As your experience grows with calling Expireds or FSBOs, you will get the feel of your prospect. Within thirty to forty-five seconds of the call, you will know which category you can put the prospect in. Understanding and respecting that the FSBO wishes to sell on their own is something we must accept. Everyone wants to save money. The more we stay in contact with them and help them along the way, the more you build layers of rapport with them. That's how we eventually earn their business.

Going After For Sale By Owners

There are different ways to find FSBOs in your area. There are different tools that I use for pulling my FSBOs, such as LANDVOICE, Mojo, and Zillow. Just so we can get to the nitty gritty, I'm assuming you already have a lead source system that provides you with leads you can prospect. I would suggest using Zillow and Craigslist for FSBOs if you are new to the business and short on funds. For this example, I will be using Zillow.

Zillow is a great way to find FSBOs. Zillow has a feature where you can select a custom radius, and when a new FSBO becomes available, the system will alert you through email. Did I mention this feature is free? You can't beat that!

The way I hunt for my FSBOs is go into the radius I set up. This area could be a few blocks, a few miles, or even include several cities. I have a fifty-mile radius selected for my prospecting area. When you're selecting your area, you want to make sure that you have a radius that you're comfortable with servicing, but not so big that it's overwhelming.

I have seen many Agents, and I admit I have done it myself, whose eyes were too big for their prospecting ability. They bit off more than they could chew in other words. It's always better to select an area where you can hyper focus rather than have a larger area where you are spread too thin. If you're spread too thin, you are ineffective, and that is just a waste of time. Remember, we are prospecting for dollars, so we must be efficient with our efforts.

Depending upon your market, you might have a few FSBOs a day, or maybe none. Just keep your eye out, and make sure you set yourself up with the FSBO alert system. You want to be constantly updated when new FSBOs become available in your area.

After a while, you may notice a trend. Some days and weeks, you may have just a few prospects, while others there is a steady wave of activity. Get in the habit of paying attention because in this business, you can get distracted very easily.

I work FSBOs quite differently than I work Expired Listings. With FSBOs, I use a manual filing system. Yes! It's just what it sounds like: I use paper. When I'm going over my new FSBOs for the day, I can see which ones make good possible leads. I print those when they first come in. It won't be long until I've generated a nice stack of high quality leads to nurture.

The advantage of a manual filing system is having all the information in front of me at once. The address, how many bedrooms and baths, the square footage, the homeowner's description of the property, year the home was built, parking, what kind of heating and cooling system are present, and if it has any major upgrades. The most important information on the page is the homeowner's contact information!

Calling the For Sale By Owner

Now you have a stack of FSBOs to call with all their information in front of you. Remember when you call, each one fits into one of three categories: appointment, follow-up, or trash. Let's start dialing!

> Hello, I'm calling about the property on 123 Main Street is this the owner.
>
> **Seller:** Yes.
>
> I see you are advertising the property as a For Sale By Owner. Is this still the case?
>
> **Seller**: Yes.
>
> OK great, how much will you take for the property?
>
> **Seller**: $300,000.

That's a good price-point for the market. What's the earliest you would like to have it sold and move by?

Seller: By January.

I can make that happen. You mentioned you're looking to sell the property for $300,000. After you pay off your loan balance and everything is said and done, how much are you looking to net to make that move by January?

Seller: $125,000.

$125,000, that sounds reasonable. If I can get you in the ballpark of $125,000 in your pocket after my fees and escrow fees are paid, would you be okay with that?

Seller: Yes.

I like to meet with people in the afternoons or on weekends. Would today at 4 work, or would 5:30 be better?

Seller: 5:30.

I would like to send you my pre-appointment package. It's basically my resume, how I sell homes, and my client testimonials. What is your best email address?

Seller: blahblah@gmail.com

Great, thank you! I'll send it over in a few minutes. So, I can be prepared for our meeting this afternoon, I would like to ask you a few quick questions. Do you have a few moments?

Seller: Yes.

You're not going to set an appointment with a FSBO all the time. The above script is a best-case scenario. In most cases, they just want to wait to see if they can do it themselves. You should be completely supportive of that notion.

Why!?!

When they finally realize it's not as easy as it seems, you have been the Agent actively following up with them. You will see how FSBO's start seeking YOU out. They will call you and say, "We tried to do it ourselves and it didn't work out. We want to list our property. When can you come by?"

The main point you need to take away is that you need to communicate with that prospect multiple times to build a rapport that includes trust. Once they have that realization, they will naturally come to you and either request or accept your services. It will take anywhere between eight and fifteen actual conversations with that prospect before you are able to convert them into an appointment.

If you have the typical conversation without setting the appointment, you want to make sure that you try your best to secure the email. That way, you can send them your pre-appointment package. Then the FSBO follow-up process begins.

The For Sale by Owner Follow-Up System

I cannot emphasize enough that you must follow up. Be creative with it. Your follow-up is an essential part of your survival as a Real Estate Agent!

1. Make the initial call. Use the script we went over earlier in this book.
2. Do your best to secure their email address.
3. During the conversation, make sure to make notes about your conversation. All the information they provide is valuable like unique attributes of the property, family history, and any unique improvements made to the property. It all qualifies as crucial information.

You can refer to these notes when you do your follow up.

4. After prospecting, send the FSBO your pre-appointment package via email.
5. After you send the email, call them and let them know you've just sent them an email with your information and they can call anytime. If they do not answer, leave a message:

"Good afternoon, this is William with Super Agent Realty. It was my privilege to speak with your earlier. I just wanted to give you a quick call to let you know that I sent over my pre-appointment package via email. If you have any questions, call me anytime at 123-456-7890. Thank you for your time."

It's as simple as that. Always keep your messages short, quick, and to the point.

6. Write a thank you card to the owner saying something like:

"Hello Mr./Mrs. Seller,

It was my privilege speaking to you the other day. You have a wonderful home, and it should sell quickly. You mentioned you had reservations about selling during the holidays. Don't worry, the holidays bring serious buyers.

If you have any questions, or you are ready to work with me, I have enclosed my business card. Call anytime. Thanks for your time and speak with you soon.

William"

7. Call them the next day to see if they have any questions regarding your pre-appointment package:

   "Good morning, Mr./Mrs. Seller, this is William with Super Agent Realty. I was just giving you a quick call to see if you received my pre-appointment package and if you had any questions."

   Seller: *Yes, we received it. Thank you, but we don't have any questions at this time.*

   No problem! I'm here if you need me. I'm assuming you have a lot of interest in the property. How many showings have you had?

   Seller: *None. 2, 6, 15 buyers looking.*

   It doesn't matter what they say, respond with this:

   "Wow, okay, that's all? You look like you have a

wonderful, unique home, Mr./Mrs. Seller. I know it will generate highly-motivated buyers. Your mentioned earlier that you were looking to move before the first of the year and that you'd like to sell for $300,000. Is that still the case?

Seller: Yes.

"If I were able to generate a buyer with a full-price offer and get you sold in the next thirty to forty-five days, would that work for you?"

Seller: I'm not looking to list my property at this time. I'm still trying to sell it on my own.

"I completely understand. Quick question: how long are you going to try to sell it on your own before you decide to work with an Agent?

Seller: Two months.

"Hey, that's sounds great, Mr./Mrs. Seller. I'll keep in touch. You have my information. If you need anything, just give me a call.

You might be thinking it's a waste of time following up when they keep on saying that they aren't interested. You must keep in mind that this is one of the building blocks of success. We made another contact with the seller. We confirmed their motivation and when they are looking to sell their property.

Always take the opportunity when it presents itself to set an appointment. Always use their motivation because **the information they give you is invaluable.**

In this example, they're looking to sell before the end of the year. They just need more time before they see how valuable we are to them.

Remember, they said for us to follow up in two months. One of rules of Real Estate is to cut that time in half. We will be staying in contact with the seller. We will establish our professionalism with consistent follow-up.

8. Call the seller on day five or six and confirm receipt of your thank you card.

"Hey Mr./Mrs. Seller. This is William May with Super Agent Realty. How are you doing this morning?"

Seller: *Doing okay. Thank you.*

"The last time we spoke, you said you were looking to move before the first of the year and

sell your home for $300,000. Is that still the case?"

Seller: Yes.

"Great! I would like to set up a time when I can come over and look at your home. I can show you how I can get your home sold faster and for more money. Would today at 4:30 work, or would 6:00 be better for your schedule?"

Seller: No. We are still going to try to sell it on our own, but thank you for the card.

"It was my pleasure, anytime. By the way, what method are you using to advertise your home?"

Seller: Oh, you know, I have a sign out front, I told my family and friends, and I posted it to Facebook. I did pretty much everything you do.

"Wow. That sounds great. How much activity are you having? Have you had any offers yet?"

Seller: No offers, but a few people are interested.

"I would suggest since you know your neighbors, conduct an Open House this *weekend. Make some flyers and knock on some doors around your neighborhood and invite seventy-five to a hundred people to your Open House. You have a wonderful home. With a little sweat equity, it will sell itself. I'll call you back in a few days to find out how things went."*

Seller: *That's a great idea! Thanks!*

I'm keeping the conversation friendly. After I ask her/him a question, I try to close the appointment. After an initial "no", I offer a valuable suggestion that also lets the owner know he/she is going to have to put in some work.

After I offer the suggestion, I leave things up to the seller. Depending on the day of the week, I may give them another call to see what the date and time of their Open House is set for. Sometimes, I will show up to the Open House toward the end. Usually, the Open House hasn't gone well, and they are happy to see me. I listen to their concerns and feel them out. Again, I try to close the appointment. If they are highly motivated, sometimes I sign the listing right then and there. **All success is continuous persistence.**

9. Follow up your suggestion with a call to see how their neighborhood door knocking went. Hopefully, it wasn't as easy as it looks, and they are ready for you to help them.
10. Continue to follow up with stubborn clients on a weekly basis. I usually contact these prospects weekly on Monday's. If they are doing any kind of prospecting for their home on their own, this usually happens on the weekends. In most cases, they are frustrated with that process. This gives you the perfect opportunity to close the appointment.
11. After a month, if it seems like the prospect is not progressing toward listing with you, put them in a folder labeled "Old FSBO Leads" in your database system.

No matter what type of prospect you are following up with, it's not difficult to stay consistent. Make sure to put prospecting in your calendar as an appointment and follow up!

For Sale by Owner Open Houses

You're probably asking yourself, "William, what do you mean by For Sale By Owner Open Houses? Are we going to help them with the Open House and hold their hand? Are we going to give them the information they need to conduct their own Open House?"

When I first heard this strategy, I had a lot of questions of my own. This is not your typical Open House. This is a focused Open House that is targeted for sellers. Yes, seller! I'm not that interested in buyers. We are looking for sellers in the community who are thinking about selling and want to work with an Agent that's going to get the job done.

Let's say that you reach an agreement with a FSBO on the terms and conditions of helping them with their Open House. There's a ton of different ways to reach an agreement regarding commission when finding a buyer. We are going to be focusing on securing homeowners who want to list now, or in the near future.

If you don't know, I'm working in Southern California. In every state, there are different laws and regulations on how you conduct your Real Estate business. You would have to check with

your own Board of Realtors in your state for guidelines on how to work out an agreement with the homeowner in this situation.

Also make sure that you are completely transparent with any buyers or potential sellers. Let them know that this is not your listing, and you're just cooperating with the homeowner and assisting them with an Open House. Always be clear, transparent, and honest about your communication with potential clients, so there will be no misunderstandings at any point!

I stress this especially, because California is the land of the lawsuit. Someone will sue you for a hangnail claiming it's your fault. Always take precautions in your business to avoid any possible confusion.

Successful Open House Game Plan

Understand we have a mission on locating, targeting, and acquiring homeowners that are thinking about selling now or in the near future. Twenty-five percent of your traffic going through an Open House are sellers thinking about selling their home. Essentially, you have multiple eyes on you: the FSBO seller, the buyers, and most of all, your potential neighborhood seller leads.

The FSBO is looking closely at your work performance and professionalism during the Open House. At the same time, they are also judging you to see how you do an Open House differently from the one they conducted, and if all went as planned. They listened to your suggestion to have their own Open House. Most likely, a civilian's Open House won't have the same effect as that of a trained, professional, Real Estate Agent.

With your Real Estate knowledge and training, your Open House will be like night and day as far as the results. They should be impressed, and see the value in hiring you as their Agent to get their home sold.

To show the FSBO seller that we're the best choice for getting their home sold, we must level-up our game plan; 10x our activities. This way, if there's any chance of them hiring us they will see our value during this Open House process.

For the best results, I would suggest planning the Open House two weeks in advance. This will give you ample time to get ready. Most sellers want things done yesterday, and this is the same with FSBO sellers. In most cases, you will only have a week or so to work with, so make sure to use your time efficiently.

Plan the Open House for a Saturday or Sunday if possible. Having a well-planned Open House over a weekend will produce the best results.

The home must be show ready! Let the seller know that for best results, the home must be ready to show before the Open House. This ensures the home is shown in its best possible shape, so you get the highest possible offers. Present them with an Open House checklist like the following:

- [ ] Declutter the entire home
- [ ] Clean the home or have it professionally cleaned
- [ ] Power wash the exterior and driveways
- [ ] Mow, touch up landscaping
- [ ] Trim trees and shrubs
- [ ] Clean the gutters
- [ ] If a pool or hot tub are present, make sure they are fresh and clean
- [ ] Clean out the garage if possible
- [ ] Remove all unnecessary vehicles from the property

These are just a few of my suggestions off my own Open House checklist. Use your own judgment and make sure the property presents itself in the best light possible.

Get the word out! Getting the word out can take several different forms. At the minimum, make sure you have a full week before your Open House. Let's assume today is Monday and your Open House starts on Saturday. The first thing we need to do is email your database about the upcoming Open House. If you are social media savvy, post to your accounts about the Open House. I recommend making three separate posts on each platform: one on Monday, another on Wednesday, and the last on Friday. Post a reminder about the Open House and let them know to bring their check books!

If you use a service like MyRealEstateTools.com, CoreFact.com, or other postcard service, consider targeting between one hundred and five hundred homes around the property and send them a postcard. Only do this if you can afford it. Don't ever spend your last dime on advertising thinking it will save you. I have been there, done that, and absolutely nothing happened. Trust me, only use marketing when you're in a good financial position to do so.

Pick up the phone! Call your database, friends, and family. Let them know you have an Open House coming up this weekend. Of course, you already emailed them, but the open rate on emails is atrocious.

It's time to circle-prospect, better known as cold calling. You need to contact one hundred to five hundred homeowners in the area and let them know the property is for sale. You're going all out.

You're going to be busy working on those calls, but don't get too busy to know the tell-tale sign of interest. If they are asking questions like how much the property is, how many bedrooms, or how many bathrooms, you are probably talking to a homeowner who is thinking about selling.

They probably won't admit it, but rest assured, they are thinking about it. One day, they're going to have that itch, and you need to keep in touch, so you can scratch it!

Keep notes, dig in, get more information! Ask questions like how long they have lived in the home, does it have major upgrades, how old is the roof, if they move, where are they looking to live? You know what you're doing. Plant that seed! When you start door knocking, you're going to make a special note to make sure you contact that homeowner. You want that **face to face, belly to belly**, conversation!

I highly suggest using a dialing system to auto-dial your calls for you. I use the Mojo Dialer from

MojoSells - http://williejmayenterprises.com/recommendations-from-william/. Something like this will make short work on the one hundred to five hundred calls you need to make. Hand-dialing will take you a long while, so if you have the means, a dialer will pay for itself in short order. That is, *if* **you make the calls!**

Go through the neighborhood twice: once at the beginning of the week, and again at the end. Your goal is to keep the Open House fresh in everyone's minds.

Hit those doors! Okay, ladies and gentlemen, it's time to roll up your sleeves and put on some comfortable shoes. We are going door-to-door! Depending upon how experienced you are with door knocking, I suggest you go through the neighborhood twice. Yes, all one hundred to five hundred homes.

It usually takes me about an hour and a half to do a hundred homes which depends greatly on how many people I talk to. I would suggest not doing more than two hundred houses in a day, especially if you're not in good shape. To hit a high quantity of doors, you must be experienced and in shape.

Choose the number of houses you will visit based on your skill level and physical condition. If you are new to door knocking and not in shape, wait until Friday and do thirty, fifty, or seventy-five homes. Hit a spot where you feel comfortable and set a goal. If you start feeling fatigued, stop and conserve your energy for the main event, your Open House!

Handouts! Okay, Agents, when you're out there in the field knocking on those doors, make sure you are giving homeowners a high-quality product. Do not give them a cheap business card or a plain black and white flyer. Make sure that whatever you're handing out is high quality. Remember, you want them to hire you and trust you with their most important asset. That is not going to happen with a black and white flyer.

Really?

I would slam the door in your face!

Seriously, when you meet these homeowners, you are basically applying for the job of representing them in the most expensive transaction they're ever going to make, so make sure you have a quality flyer. It needs to be well-designed, have a great description, and outstanding photos.

You want this flyer to be printed on high-gloss, 100-pound paper. One side should have the information about the property, and the other side should offer them something of value such as an instant home evaluation, your contact information, and offer to answer any questions they may have. Make it catchy and include a call to action. They will either call you or go to your website.

Once you identify that they have interest and are thinking about selling their property, they stay on your radar until they list, die, or tell you stop contacting them. We will talk about this more when we discuss your database.

When I pass out flyers, I wrap them around a notepad. They might keep the flyer, but even if they toss it, my notepad will become part of the family. It will play Gin Rummy, Dominoes, or go along to the supermarket. My notepads even go to church and help take notes on the Sunday service. **Notepads have stickability.**

I can't tell you how many times I've been door knocking in my farm area and had someone chase me down for another notepad, or call me and request another one. There's a little secret out there that not too many coaches will tell you: **notepads are the secret weapon on winning a farm area.**

Notepads are a tool to help you stay in front of the

client. If you're financially strapped and you can't purchase flyers, check with your Lender to see if you can work out a partnership where they cover the flyers on their end. Be sure and check with your brokerage first to ensure you are not breaking any rules or regulations.

Check on the property the day before the Open House. While you are running around like a crazy person, stop by the property to make sure the Open House checklist has been completed and everything is to your liking.

Game on! Open House Day! You should be excited. Your hard work and determination will show today. Just a few more housekeeping details to make sure the day goes off without a hitch.

Expect a full house. Depending upon the amount of traffic you are expecting, you should have a two-person team working your Open House. I would suggest that team be made up of you and a Lender. That way you can transform the Open House into a one-stop shop. Having a Lender will help you manage the potential clients coming in and help you screen potential buyers that are pre-qualified, as well as those who are not.

This is completely up to you, but I think it's a good idea to set up an agreement with a good Buyer's

Agent that will agree to pay you a 25% referral fee for any buyers you refer and they close escrow with. That percentage is just an example, it can be any percentage the two of you can agree on. Our main goal is to acquire listings, FSBO listings, and listings from the community.

A few hours before the event, put up fifteen to thirty signs around the neighborhood advertising your Open House. There are companies you can hire to do this for you or you can have your Buyer's Agent take care of the job. Have a lot of signs everywhere. This is a 10x Open House, it's MEGA! Whatever you call it, if you're serious about producing listings for your business before the holidays, we are stepping up our game. This system can be used for any Open House and it will generate listings and passive referral income from the Buyer's Agent.

Arrive at the Open House a minimum of an hour before it begins. This will give you plenty of time should anything unexpected pop up.

Picture it: You have signs all over the neighborhood with the tall banners, signs, and flags out front. Just before the Open House begins, BBQ Pete's smoking, joking, catering truck pulls up and starts blowing barbecue smoke all over the neighborhood. You invited all the neighbors over for free barbecue and to check out the Open House.

You don't have to do the catering truck, but in Los Angeles, they're not that expensive. There are so many options with the trucks. Some are health food, Mexican, Italian, and the list goes on. If you can imagine it, there's probably a catering truck for it. You can also go the traditional route, and offer a simple spread of wine, cheese, cookies, or whatever you are comfortable with.

Dress the part! Dress to impress, ladies and gentlemen. No white shirts and flip flops. You are directly paid on your level of professionalism including your attire, so look and present yourself professionally. Don't go to late-night parties the night before. In fact, go to bed early so you are on the very top of your game.

Sign them in! Have a sign-in sheet (or an iPad) at the door so you can grab the information of these potential clients as they come in. Let them know that once they sign in and their information is verified, you will give them a voucher for the catering truck. You will have some who don't want to sign in no matter what. Let them know that the homeowner has requested that everyone sign in for safety reasons. If they are represented by an Agent, receiving the

Agent's business card will suffice for sign-in for me, but it's up to you how you want to handle that.

TIP: Always be professional. Don't give buyers who come in with an Agent the cold shoulder. Answer all their questions and be sure to give them vouchers for the catering truck especially. You are running a small business here, and if you treat potential clients unprofessionally, that will get around through the grapevine. Even though you're in competition with other Agents in your area, you should always help them out. Set the example.

Once things are in full swing, and you're seeing some traction, that is the perfect time to pull out your phone and do a Facebook Live video with an app called Live Leap - http://williejmayenterprises.com/recommendations-from-william/. This app syndicates your Facebook Live to your own Page, Group, and other places on Facebook you want to share the video. Send the video to the seller's Timeline! All their friends and family will see the Mega Open House you've put together and they will be crazy not to hire you. Look at the magnitude of work you've put in to show them that you are different!

Don't sit down! During this event, you must interact with people. If people are coming up the house, go out and greet them! This is not your typical Open House, we are on the hunt for sellers! Be familiar with the area, the types of homes in the area, the local school district, what is the highest priced home that sold in the neighborhood. Do your homework, so when you meet those potential sellers, they will see you as an authority on the neighborhood even if they've never seen you before. This will help you establish a connection with them.

Here's a script for interacting with potential sellers:

With confidence:

Good afternoon! Welcome to our Open House today. My name is William May. What's yours?

Potential Seller: Mr./Mrs. Joe Buyer/Mr./Mrs. Joe Seller.

Nice to meet you, [insert name here]. I know you probably have a few questions about the house and neighborhood, so let me tell you about the house, and maybe I can answer some of the other questions you have.

This is a Craftsman-style home with an open floor plan. There are four bedrooms with two and a half baths. There is a little over 2,100 square feet of living space with a 10,000-square foot lot. The home has central air and heating. It was built in 1997.

Since then, the home has had only one owner. It is in a very prestigious neighborhood called Circle Hills Estates. If you don't mind me asking, how did you hear about the Open House?

If you noticed from the script, I do several things here that you should take note of. Seriously, if you have this book, feel free to scribble in the margins. If you are listening on Audible or reading the eBook, make sure you're taking notes in a way that's comfortable for you.

I am interacting with a potential client with confidence and authority. I have demonstrated my market knowledge of the neighborhood. I have done my homework. You do not want to be one of those Agents when someone asks one of the following questions and you can't answer:

1. How old is the roof?
2. Any major upgrades?
3. What are the schools like?
4. What school district is this?

"I don't know" is a bad answer that will not earn you any business. It can take a bit of practice, but if you put the time in, you will become better and better at it. You will be scared and nervous at first, but the more you do it, the better you will become.

If you are speaking with buyers, they will see that you know what you are talking about. With the information you've initially provided, you have already answered the most common buyer questions. If you are speaking with a seller, they will already know most of the answers, but this is a great opportunity to impress them when they see you know your stuff.

If they are thinking about selling, they are going to naturally gravitate toward you because you are knowledgeable. That's exactly what we want! We want to win over sellers.

Their answer to your question is very important. If they say they learned about the Open House through your signs, then you know the number of signs you put out is good. If they say Internet, that is good because it means your social media, Craigslist post, or Zillow advertisements regarding your Open House are working well. If they say they received your personal invitation through your door-knocking campaign, then you can take that as a slam dunk. They know you mean business and you are producing results. Your job, no matter what kind of prospect they are, is to qualify them and see how you can help.

On the side note: You must consider that your Open House signs, banners, flags and Mr. Pete's BBQ catering truck is enhancing your Open House success rate exponentially. You're using their senses to entice them. Think about that for a second. All your Open House signs and the smell of barbecue in the air is like leading a mouse to cheese. It looks like a party and the curiosity is thick. It makes people want to pull up and check out the Open House. That is exactly why this works.

You don't have to go to this level, but you get the idea. If you've been in the business for any length of time, you know that Open Houses generally do not sell homes. The Agent activity sells the house. After everything has been said and done, your Buyer's Agent picks up the signs, your Lender closes shop for the day with a ton of leads you both generated.

The seller will inevitably say, "This was a long day, we had a lot of traffic, but I didn't get an offer on my home."

Here is what you say to that:

"Mr./Mrs. Seller, you see how I work. If you want to get your home sold, I could come back tomorrow with my eighteen-point marketing plan and show you exactly how I can get your home sold for top dollar while doing all the work for you. Would tomorrow at 1:00 work or would 2:00 be better for your schedule?"

After the Open House, you should have generated a good quantity of leads. Have your Lender and the Buyer's Agent work with the buyer leads. As a precaution, remind them to contact those leads that night or the following day to follow up so they do not forget you. Make sure they follow up!

At the same time, some of those leads were sellers who might need to sell and then purchase another home soon, so make sure you nurture those leads in your database. Contact them the same day or the following day. Thank them for taking the time to come out and see the Open House. Let them know that if there's anything they need, they can give you a call anytime. Send them a thank you card and follow up with them according to their motivation to sell.

Remember, there are no guarantees with anything I teach in this book, but with this strategy, it's highly possible to generate very good buyer and seller leads. Try it out and let me know about your experience by emailing me at william@williejmayenterprises.com.

Past Clients, SOI, and Your Database

Merry Christmas and Happy New Year! One of the best parts of having a successful business in Real Estate, is having a referral-based business. People who know you, like you and trust you. Your friends, family, neighbors, mechanic, plumber, doctor, lawyer, pastor, and babysitter; these people are your raving fans. They like you, care about you, and if you have that award-winning personality, they may even love you!

They are going to refer business to you. It's not a coincidence when you listen to interviews by top producers. One of the main sources of their business are referrals. Have you asked yourself why that is? Let me give you something to think about to put it into perspective. Have you ever referred somebody to your place of work? Has someone ever referred you to theirs simply because they cared about you and your well-being?

It's the same with Real Estate. If your friends, family, and past clients care about you and your business, they're going to do whatever they can to support you and your business. That's why so many Agents are attracted to a referral-based business. To have a successful, referral-based business, you must make contact with your past clients, SOI, and your database.

To simplify the system and make it easy for you, we are just going to integrate all three forms of clients into one. We'll just call it, you guessed it, your database! Let's get to work.

Creating Your Database

Just in case you're a brand-new Agent or an Agent that has never worked your database, I'll show you how to build your database from the ground up. Let's start by using your cell phone. How many contacts do you have in your phone? A hundred? Five hundred? A thousand? Whatever the number, that is a good place to start. You need a good contact management system inside a customer relations manager or CRM to manage your contacts with ease.

In my last book, *Top 10 Expired Objections*, I mentioned that I use two CRMs:

- Mojo Dialer
- Contactually

You can find out more about both on my website - http://williejmayenterprises.com/recommendations-from-william/.

I still use both, but for this chapter, I going to focus on Contactually.

Full disclosure: as of this writing, I do not get paid from this company. I truly believe this CRM is a good and easy way to keep in constant contact with your database. Contactually also includes an accountability feature that I really appreciate.

Integrating your contacts into Contactually is very easy and seamless. For example, if you have Gmail, it's as easy as logging into your Gmail account in the Contactually system and letting it import all your contacts. Voila! One of the best features that I love about Contactually is that it updates the contact information each time you email them, send a text message, or call them. All your communication is visible in the database. Did I mention that I love this feature?

Contactually has so many systems and resources, there is no way I can cover them all, but once you import your contacts, there is a cool game where you sort all your contacts into different buckets. The game is called the Bucket Game. You can customize each bucket with a name, frequency, and to-do list. For example, you might have one where contacts in that bucket start an 8x8 system that you created.

Also, I have trouble with names sometimes, and Contactually has an option where you can include a picture of your contact in their profile. This is so helpful to me because it helps me remember that contact on a deeper level. When I call them, I can remember what they look like.

If you're not comfortable with any of the multiple line dialers out there, I have a solution for you: Kixie.

It's a wonderful program that's not that expensive. You can click to call your clients, and it integrates seamlessly with Contactually. It also integrates with several other database systems. You can make and receive calls, have your calls recorded, text message, drop pre-recorded voicemails, and it automatically updates your database with a log and more.

If you're interested and would like to learn more, email Kixie at: hello@kixie.com. In the subject line, type: William May Referral. Simply let them know you were referred by me. You will receive a fourteen-day trial with no credit card required. See a video of it in action -

https://www.youtube.com/watch?v=XX2Hoo_DBsQ.

With Kixie or without, Contactually's system is very robust. I would suggest you go to the website and check out their tutorials. You will fall in love with it. If this is not your cup of tea, the systems I'm going to share with you can be used with any other contact management system that you feel comfortable with.

Who do we put in our database? We want to make sure that we get everybody we know into our new database. This list includes immediate and extended family, friends, church, neighborhood watch, social groups like Facebook, current and past clients, your vendor list, mechanic, doctor, lawyer, escrow officer, and so on. Understand this is going to be the lifeblood of your business. Remember if they have a pulse and they like you, they go in your database.

Vendor List
Make sure you create a vendors list. A vendor list is essential to your business and the relationship that you build with your clients. Life happens so it is always best to be prepared. If you have a good electrician, plumber, handyman, or painter that you can refer your clients to, it will make you look like a hero. When you help your clients out of a situation, that pays dividends in the long run.

Their Ideal Information

Obviously, we want to pack as much information in their profile as possible including, but not limited to: first and last name, relationship, address, email, telephone number, description of your relationship, birthday, anniversaries, kids, and their pet's favorite food. I'm not saying go as far as getting their blood type, but if you can add it into your database, do it.

You will not be able to get all this valuable information on the first call. You will retrieve it through a series of interactions with your client by listening. The more you listen, the more rapport and trust you build with your contacts. It's a continuous exercise, at least for me, not to talk so much during the conversation. I must remember to listen 80% of the time and speak 20% of the time. That is when opportunities present themselves.

For example, you have a conversation with a client and they mention their son's sixteenth birthday in June which is a few months away. This gives you the perfect opportunity to send a birthday card with some sort of gift card inside. You mail that off a week and a half before June, and you follow up with them the first part of June to see if they received your birthday card. You give them a call, that's if they don't call you first. Little steps like these, help build an unbreakable rapport with your clients that no other Agent can compete with.

If you want to step up your game to the next level I suggest you use Send Out Cards. Send Out Cards is very easy to use. You can customize gift cards and greeting cards. You can also send all sorts of gifts. Check out my interview with Gayle Zientek, the Send Out Card Queen - https://youtu.be/eHW5XxDdzpQ

In this interview, we go deep into showing you how to use the system and how to use it to follow up. If you would like to get signed up.
check out this link -
http://williejmayenterprises.com/sendoutcards.

The FORD Technique

One of the best passive ways to get most of all the information you need from your client is to use the FORD technique in regular conversation. This is a great technique if you are nervous about calling your past clients or sphere of influence. It gives you a system to start and continue a conversation where if you did not use this technique, you would just be holding the phone looking silly. No one likes having those awkward conversations.

That's why I like to use the FORD technique so much. Before I used this technique, I was so scared about picking up the phone. I always had to do something other than having a conversation with someone because I was so scared. I was suffering from **avoidance behavior,** I was doing busy work instead of prospecting.

The thing is, the more I picked up the phone, and talked to people while practicing the FORD technique, the more comfortable I became on the phone. The effects spilled over into my personal interactions as well with family, friends, and just starting conversations with people.

Since I know my scripts and I use the FORD technique, it has helped with my cold calling exponentially. In the first six months of 2017, I called more than 100,000 numbers and talked to 6,000 people. You cannot reach that level if you are scared to talk to people.

You have heard this many times before, and I never believed it myself, "If I can do it, you can definitely do it!"

I believe now because I'm not crippled by not knowing what to say. I always know what to say. I take time to practice and rehearse, and because of this simple technique, so can you!

The Ford Technique is outlined as follows:

Family
Occupation
Recreation
Dreams

F Stands for Family

Family is always a great topic of discussion. Who doesn't want to talk about their family? If you are talking to your clients, they love talking about their kids. Little Johnny just made it into Little League, their daughter, Jessica, just got a scholarship to a prestigious college, or their grandkids are growing up like little weeds. People are proud of their kids.

If you put your mind to it, there's a hundred and one topics of discussion, but always remember to keep the conversation light, simple, and easy. Never ask personal questions or questions regarding gossip. Never go down the rabbit hole of negativity. Always focus on the positives.

Here are a few examples you can ask regarding their family:

1. How long has your family been living in this neighborhood?
2. Are you originally from Houston, Texas?
3. How did you meet your wife?
4. How is your family?
5. How are your children?
6. What's your dog's name? (Yes of course, dogs are family too!)

O Stands for Occupation

Talking about their occupation can be interesting. Your clients can either have a job or a career. In any case, they probably know a lot about the field they work in. This makes this topic of discussion very interesting because many times I've learned things about a career I did not know. At the same time, it lets your client feel that you truly are interested in them, their career, and their well-being.

Here are a few examples you can ask regarding their occupation:

1. What attracted you to your present career?
2. What do you like most about your career?
3. How long have you been in your present career?
4. Do you have family and friends that are interested in your career?

TIP: Do not ask questions about money or salary. The only exception to the rule with this is if they're able to buy a property. The best practice is to have your preferred Lender handle this discussion.

R Stands for Recreation

Recreation could be a wide range of things such as sports, movies, or vacations. Dig in and see what kind of fun activities they like to get involved in or use to unwind. Maybe they like going to the movies during the weekends with the kids. Maybe after a hard day's work, they like to relax by reading a good book. When you find similarities between what you like and what your clients like, this helps the conversation and the bonding process.

Here are a few examples you can ask regarding recreation:

1. Have any vacation plans in the near future?
2. What do you do for fun?
3. How is your favorite sports team doing?
4. What is your favorite book?
5. Have you seen any good movies lately?

If you find you and your client have similar interests, expound on that, and take notes for future conversations.

D Stands for Dreams

I always like talking to people about their dreams. Their dreams can be anything from starting a new business to seeing their children graduate from college. It could even be a simple weight loss goal before their 20th reunion. You really find out about a person on a deeper level when they share what their main goals in life are. When you take interest in what they care about and support them, believe me, this means the world to them.

Here are a few examples you can ask regarding their dreams:

1. If money was no object, where in the world would you travel to?
2. You said you were going to go back to school, what would you take up?
3. Have you ever thought about writing a book, and if so, what about?
4. When you retire what are your plans? Will you travel the world or maybe road trip?
5. Where is the most exotic place you ever traveled, and would you do it again?

As I said before, the more you communicate with people and use the FORD technique, the better communicator you become. Every time you're touching your database, make sure that you have a notepad or scratchpad, so you can take notes. Later, put those notes in your database.

Remember, let them talk 80% of the time while you only talk 20% of the time. You should mostly be asking questions. Listen, learn, and take notes. Always smile when you talk to your clients. It's crazy but they can hear your smile through the phone and that passes on your positive energy. I hope I'm not the only one that can hear somebody smiling over the phone.

Your Year-Round Follow-Up Plan

We are going to start off with one hundred contacts in your database. More is better, but for this example, we are going to start with a hundred for the sake of easy math. These contacts are a mixture of past clients, sphere of influence, and vendors. Like I said before, if they have a pulse and they like you, then they should be in your database.

The point of staying in contact with everyone is so you always stay in the front of their mind when they, or someone they know, needs any sort of Real Estate service.

The 5-Step System

This 5-step system is one you need to use on a continuous basis. I dare you to find any top-producing Agent that bases their business on referrals. They will confirm that they stay in front of their database consistently. This is proven with Realtors across the country, day in and day out.

The bonus of working with your database is dealing with people that care about you, like you, trust you, are past clients, and people with whom you work. The conversations flow more freely and there's not anxiety when you pick up the phone to call them because you know what to say.

Even if it's been a while since you spoke with them, it's not a big deal because you are going to implement this follow-up system and get back in touch with the people who matter most: your database.

Email

Send out an email of pertinent information to your database bi-weekly. That's around twenty-six emails per year.

One tool I use is Google Alerts - https://www.google.com/alerts. I have it set up so I get an update once a week on the California Real Estate market. On the second Sunday of each month, I do a Bomb Bomb video speaking on Real Estate news that I have received from Google Alerts, or some other topic that I think would interest my clients.

With Bomb Bomb - http://williejmayenterprises.com/recommendations-from-william/ - I can schedule my videos for release on Monday morning to my database. Making and syndicating the videos only takes me a few minutes. The most effective thing about this method is to be consistent. Several of my clients have told me that they look forward to my video reports.

I use Corefact - http://williejmayenterprises.com/recommendations-from-william/ - the last week of the month to send everyone a neighborhood update with homes that recently sold during that month. I get notified when they open the attachment. Wouldn't you like to get notified each time someone is curious about the value of their home? I would!

The best things about sending out a localized market update is reaching homeowners who are on the fence about selling. When they receive your market update, it reminds them that they have another mortgage payment in a few days. The information you send might be just enough to knock them off that fence and list with you. **Follow-up is the key to success!**

There are many different email companies out there. Experiment and see which one works best for you.

Snail Mail

I love to send out a postcard once a month to my clients. I use My Real Estate Tools - http://williejmayenterprises.com/recommendations-from-william/ - and one of their products that I enjoy are the monthly postcards. I put my database on a campaign and have never had a problem with their system. The monthly postcard campaign is designed to stay in front of your database with your branding, your face, and your business. I've never had to worry about breaking the bank with My Real Estate Tools as they are very affordable.

You can also use Send Out Cards, and send them a custom card. Whatever you decide to use, the goal is to be the Agent they mention any time they think of Real Estate services.

Phone Calls

Set your contact management system to call your database every sixty days. When we cover the fourth quarter follow-up plan, you will up your game for keeping in touch with your clients over the holidays.

Always have the mindset that these are easy calls to make. Don't let the drunken monkey tell you anything different even if you haven't spoken to someone in a few years. You are calling them now, and that's all that matters.

Here's a quick script for calling someone you haven't talked to in a long time:

Hello, Mr./Mrs. Past Client. It's amazing how time flies, how have you been? Wow, that's wonderful. How is the family?

That's amazing how kids grow these days. How's everything at work?

Congratulations on your promotion! The last time we spoke, you said you were working on the backyard to create a relaxation area. How is that coming along?

Sounds wonderful! I'm going to have to pop by one day soon. Do you have any vacation plans in the near future?

Mr./Mrs. Past Client, it's always a privilege talking to you. If you ever need me, give me a call. Have a great day.

Always take notes when you have a conversation. This is useful for your follow-up calls. Send them a thank you card that same day. If you like Send Out Cards, this is the perfect situation to send out a custom card congratulating them on their promotion or whatever is going on in life.

If you are friends on Facebook, you can always take a picture from their Timeline to further customize your card. For example, say they got a new puppy, you can send out a card saying, "It was good speaking with you the other day. Congratulations on your new family member. Have a great day, and I'll speak with you soon."

All these contacts, or touches and interactions, are building up like a compound effect. You are slowly building a powerhouse of referrals one client at a time.

Pop By

I love to pop by my client's homes. You should go by once every three months. Don't stay long and bring something of value like a notepad, market update, or simple gift. If you need ideas, visit Brian Buffini's website - https://www.buffiniandcompany.com/pbt.htm. He has a ton of pop-by gift ideas. **There is nothing like belly to belly, and face to face in Real Estate.** If you're taking the time to show up at the front door just to check in because you're in the neighborhood, that puts you in a different category of relationship.

For example, I was knocking on doors in my farm area, passing out my newsletter and notepads, when

I came across a homeowner who asked me if I knew a good plumber. I do have a couple I deal with, so I told them I could get them the info in an hour or so. I asked for their best phone number, and once I received it, I asked for their email as well. I told the homeowner that I had a list of vendors that I work with that includes electricians, plumbers, and handymen. I asked if that would be a list of value to her, and she said, "Yes!"

So, I sent her the information via email and called to verify that she received it. Then, I put her in my database just as I'm telling you to do. To make a long story short, she already had a family Realtor that sold her a home, but because I was there for her, I follow up, and pop by at least once a quarter, I am her Real Estate Agent of choice now. I built a relationship over time, and face-to-face is the best way to accomplish that.

This is an easy system, but most Agents have a hard time staying with it. What I have found most effective for me is that I check my calendar the Sunday night before my week starts. Let's say I have five pop-bys for that week. I can knock that out early Saturday morning when most people are home.

I use an app called Road Warrior Route Planner - https://roadwarriorllc.com on my phone. It is amazing!

I have been in transportation for over twenty-five years. I owned my own school bus company, and I must say this app is one of the best and simplest to use in my opinion. It works for Android or iOS. You just input all your addresses that you are going to hit that day, tap **Optimize**, and in a few short seconds, it plans out your route synced with your phone's GPS. By default, it plans the shortest possible route. It's a huge time-saver.

Special Dates

When we work our database, we are going to:

1. Email them bi-weekly.
2. Send them snail mail once per month.
3. Call them every other month. If they don't answer, leave a message.
4. Every three months you need to grace your database with your presence.

So that's four, what is the fifth system?

Special dates.

Every client in your database should have special dates for their birthday, their children's birthdays, wedding anniversaries, anniversary of their home purchase, and any other date of significance. They should all be in your calendar.

For example, let's say you have a client who purchases a home. You do active follow-up with that client according to this system. They know you, they like you, they trust you, and they love you because you've stayed in contact with them. When most Agents would have called it "job done", you're still in the game!

It is the month of the anniversary of the purchase of their home, so you send them an updated CMA on their property, a custom anniversary card from Send Out Cards, and a handwritten letter. Depending upon your schedule, drop by their home within a few days of their anniversary or on the day of, and congratulate them. This will turn your database clients into raving fans. When it comes time for them to sell their home, they will come to you because you demonstrated your value to them consistently and persistently.

This is just one example of custom dates. This might sound crazy, but your database is a living, breathing system that needs constant attention because it is the life source of your business. If you don't take care of your database, it will die, and then your business will die. Without it, you can't generate new business. If your business is stagnant or dying, it is because you have not been working your database, or worse, you don't have a database.

The good news is, if you have a database, you can begin working it today! If you don't have one, you can start building one right now! Don't wait. If you are interested in your financial future, I suggest that you start working on your database as soon as possible.

Final Thoughts

As you know, October 1st is the start of our Fourth Quarter, and the beginning of the end of the year. The deals you take right now, will determine your Christmas and New Year and how you start the following year. Somewhere around November 15th will be the last day you can take a traditional Escrow to close before the end of the year. Yes, I know, if you have a good lender you can close within thirty days or so, but I like working with the worst case scenario. That's why I chose forty-five days.

I would like to tell you right now, thank you for purchasing my book. This book will not do you any good if you don't utilize the information within it. Do not let this book sit on your shelf and collect dust. Use this book as your Real Estate Survival Guide for the holidays. Not only for the holidays, these tactics are your year-round Real Estate Survival Guide.

A successful Real Estate Agent can make more than most doctors, lawyers, and even surgeons. We have a license to sell. If you work smart, hard, and are consistent with your prospecting, the sky's the limit. I read in Forbes Magazine that the highest paid salespeople, "sell with a purpose" or "sell with a noble purpose". They are not selling to get rich or famous, but to help people. What is your purpose when you are selling Real Estate? What is your WHY?

Whatever your purpose is, let that drive you towards success, have it yank you out of bed in the morning, and allow it to destroy self-doubt and avoidance behavior. Let it guide you through your prospecting calls during the day. Depending on the individual, it takes anywhere from sixty to seventy-five days to develop a habit. Studies have shown once that habit is ingrained in you, even if you don't want to do it, your inner drive will compel you to continue doing it. There have been times when I did not want to go to the office and prospect, but I was so conditioned on doing it. I still went. Once I was on the phone making calls, I was glad I came in.

Your habit will drive you when the days of your fire and passion run low. I believe in you. You have it in yourself to be a successful Real Estate Agent. I know I talk a lot about mindset throughout this book, but sometimes we need a kick in the pants. If you let that drunken monkey in your mind to control your success, you will never succeed.

So if you need a little help fighting the drunken monkey, practicing your scripts and dialogues, or you would just like to mastermind with other Real Estate Agents, I have started a new Facebook group called

Real Estate Agents That Hustle - https://www.facebook.com/groups/RealEstateAgentsThatHustle/. I invite you to join us, so we can help you mold your Real Estate career for success.

I would like to congratulate you for taking the time out of your busy schedule to read this book. I really appreciate it. I know many Agents struggle in Real Estate, myself included. I wanted to put together something that will benefit fellow Agents and their families.

As I stated in the beginning of this book, the Christmas season is my favorite time of the year. If I can give you the information that helped me in my business and help you in yours, that would be the best Christmas present for me and my family. I hope and pray that the information in this book will increase your business tenfold. If it has, please contact me and let me know. No matter where you are in the world, what race or religion, no matter what language you speak, I want to hear from you. From the bottom of my heart, from my family to yours, Merry Christmas and Happy New Year. May God richly bless you.

If you enjoyed this book:

Please check out my first book: *Top 10 Expired Objections.* Available exclusively from Amazon. Grab the link on my website - http://williejmayenterprises.com/

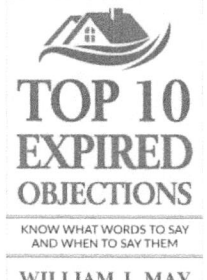

www.ingramcontent.com/pod-product-compliance
Lightning Source LLC
Chambersburg PA
CBHW070259230526
45470CB00002B/649